INTRODUCTION

Reading is an exciting challenge for the young learner. Though the student is eager to learn new skills, the path along the way can be intimidating. This book is designed to give encouragement and to reinforce the learning process with successful experiences. Rebus puzzles introduce new words to the students in a fun and playful way. Students then gain more familiarity with the new words through the activities and game provided.

The pages in this book introduce new vocabulary words in the form of rebus pictures. The new word will appear in a short selection as a rebus picture beside its written form. In the next selection, one of the rebus words appears in written form without the rebus picture. Unit activities, as well as the game on pages 31 and 32, repeat exposure to the written forms.

Each unit in *Rebus Puzzles* is designed so that the students can make small booklets. You may wish to photocopy story pages individually and give them to the students at reading time. Provide folders to store the pages. After all the pages have been read, the students can staple together and color the pages before taking them home to share with a family member.

USE

To begin, determine the implementation that best fits your students' needs and your classroom structure. The following plan is one suggested format.

- Introduce: Tell the students they will learn the written words for things that they already know. Explain that you will read a story aloud and that they will follow along on their own. As you encounter a rebus picture, you will pause, and together, the students can say the word indicated by the picture. They can immediately make a connection from the rebus picture to the written word.

  As you progress to the next selection, the picture for one of the new words will appear in its written form without the rebus picture beside it. You can again pause as you approach the word, allowing the students to remember the word or refer to the previous selection for a rebus picture reminder. Then, the students can say the word aloud.

- Activity Pages: Give the students a copy of the activity page. Let the students know that the activities on the page will be fun as well as helpful. Explain how to complete the page.

- Pretest and Posttest: The pretests and posttests can be administered before each unit is read and after the activity is completed. You and the students can gauge the progress they have made.

ADDITIONAL IDEAS

- Individual Progress Sheet: The chart provided on page 3 is a recording device to help maintain a master list of individual student progress. As you observe each student's accomplishment of a task, record the date she or he completed it.

- Game: A game appears at the end of this book as a review of the new words. It can be mounted on construction paper, cut out, and stored for easy management. Copies could be made for each student and sent home for further reinforcement.

WORD LIST

Below is a list of the words that the students will master after completing *Rebus Puzzles*. The numeral following each word refers to the page on which the rebus word is introduced to the students.

Unit 1: The Very Best Pet

beak	7
bench	9
bowl	6
cage	6
castle	10
dolphin	10
eagle	7
gerbil	6
goldfish	10
ladder	7
lizard	8
monkey	5
park	5
parrot	7
plug	10
purse	9
rain	9
school	5
shell	8
swing	7
table	6
tank	8
toad	8
umbrella	9
zoo	5

Unit 2: To See the World

basket	19
beach	19
blanket	19
boots	15
chair	14
crown	18
elephant	17
firefighter	18
flashlight	16
gloves	15
grasshopper	14
hose	18
lion	17
mountains	15
octopus	16
seahorse	16
shark	16
sled	15
tiger	17
vine	17
volcano	18
wave	19
world	14
yo-yo	14
zebra	17

Unit 3: Things to Do

balloons	25
basketball	24
bowling	24
candle	28
carrots	23
clouds	28
clown	25
cookies	23
flute	27
football	24
guitar	27
harp	27
horn	27
horse	25
juice	25
lightning	28
piano	27
plane	26
potato	23
rainbow	28
sailboat	26
soccer	24
spoon	23
tractor	26
truck	26

Student's Name ______________________________

INDIVIDUAL PROGRESS SHEET

Fill in the completion date for the student for each task.

Unit 1	Participates in reading story	Reads word with rebus	Reads word without rebus	Unit 2	Participates in reading story	Reads word with rebus	Reads word without rebus	Unit 3	Participates in reading story	Reads word with rebus	Reads word without rebus
1. beak				26. basket				51. balloons			
2. bench				27. beach				52. basketball			
3. bowl				28. blanket				53. bowling			
4. cage				29. boots				54. candle			
5. castle				30. chair				55. carrots			
6. dolphin				31. crown				56. clouds			
7. eagle				32. elephant				57. clown			
8. gerbil				33. firefighter				58. cookies			
9. goldfish				34. flashlight				59. flute			
10. ladder				35. gloves				60. football			
11. lizard				36. grasshopper				61. guitar			
12. monkey				37. hose				62. harp			
13. park				38. lion				63. horn			
14. parrot				39. mountains				64. horse			
15. plug				40. octopus				65. juice			
16. purse				41. seahorse				66. lightning			
17. rain				42. shark				67. piano			
18. school				43. sled				68. plane			
19. shell				44. tiger				69. potato			
20. swing				45. vine				70. rainbow			
21. table				46. volcano				71. sailboat			
22. tank				47. wave				72. soccer			
23. toad				48. world				73. spoon			
24. umbrella				49. yo-yo				74. tractor			
25. zoo				50. zebra				75. truck			

Name ______________________ Date ______________

Look at the words.
Circle things you find outside.
Underline things that need to eat food.
Put a ★ star by things you find inside.
Draw a box around one thing you find on a bird.
Words may be used more than one time.

PET STORE

beak		rain
bench		school
bowl	ladder	shell
cage	lizard	swing
castle	monkey	table
dolphin	park	tank
eagle	parrot	toad
gerbil	plug	umbrella
goldfish	purse	zoo

See the Answer Key on page 33.

Name ______________________________ Date ______________

The Teacher's Pet

Greg, Leo, and Shondra were friends. They walked home from school together. One day, they went to the park. They liked to play together in the park.

"I think our teacher, Mrs. Thomas, wants a pet," said Greg. "I saw her at the pet store. I hope she will get a pet monkey."

"She might get a pet," said Shondra. "I do not think she will get a monkey. Mrs. Thomas once said she liked a monkey in the zoo. She will not have one at home!"

Leo's Guess

Mrs. Thomas told the children some news. "I went to the pet store," she said. "I will have a new pet soon. It doesn't make any noise. It can fit in a small place. It doesn't eat a lot. Can you guess what it is?"

Leo said, "I think it is a gerbil. It is little and doesn't eat a lot. It is not very loud. A monkey can be too loud!"

"Yes," said Greg. "A gerbil will need a cage. It will need a bowl for food. It could live on the table in a cage. We know what pet it is!"

Shondra's Guess

The children enjoyed guessing what Mrs. Thomas's new pet would be.

Shondra said, "I think Mrs. Thomas's new pet will be a parrot. She said that the bird she likes the best is an eagle. I think that a parrot could fit in a cage. An eagle cannot fit. A parrot could climb up a little ladder. It will talk to her every day."

"A parrot can even climb with its beak," said Leo. "The beak is very strong."

"Yes," said Shondra. "Mrs. Thomas could get it a little swing, too. A parrot is the best pet for Mrs. Thomas!"

Greg's Guess

The children kept guessing what kind of pet Mrs. Thomas would get.

"Mrs. Thomas can't trick me," Greg said. "She told us that her little pet won't make any noise. A parrot will talk too much. A lizard won't make a sound. A lizard could live in a fish tank. But there will be no water in this fish tank. It will have just a small bowl of water for drinking."

"Yes," Leo said. "It can have some friends, too. A turtle is a good friend. It can live in the tank, too. It can hide in its shell if it is shy."

Greg said, "A toad would be another good friend for this lizard. Mrs. Thomas can have lots of pets."

The New Pet

Mrs. Thomas went to the pet store the next day. She saw the children sitting on a bench. She asked them for help.

"I will hold my purse. Will you carry my boxes?" she asked.

The children were happy to help her. The rain began to fall. Mrs. Thomas held up her umbrella for everyone. They were all glad that it was a very big umbrella.

Greg said, "We have tried to guess what kind of pet you will get. I think you will get a lizard. Will we find out today?"

"Yes," said Mrs. Thomas. "Today is the day! We will take these boxes into my house. Then, you will see my new pet."

Good Friends

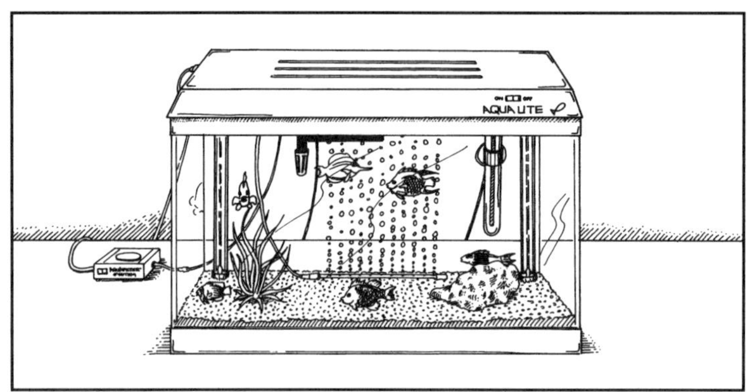

Mrs. Thomas set her purse on the table. The children put the boxes down, too. Mrs. Thomas opened the first box.

"A fish tank!" cried Leo.

Mrs. Thomas opened another box. "This is a bubble maker. Greg, will you find the plug, please?"

"Yes, I will," said Greg. "Did you get a baby dolphin?" he asked.

"I wonder," said Mrs. Thomas. She opened another box. Out came a little castle.

"Shondra, please set this in the fish tank."

At last, out of the last box came the pet.

"A goldfish!" cried the children.

"Yes. My new goldfish will be a good friend for me," said Mrs. Thomas. "You children are good friends for me, too!"

Name ______________________ Date ______________

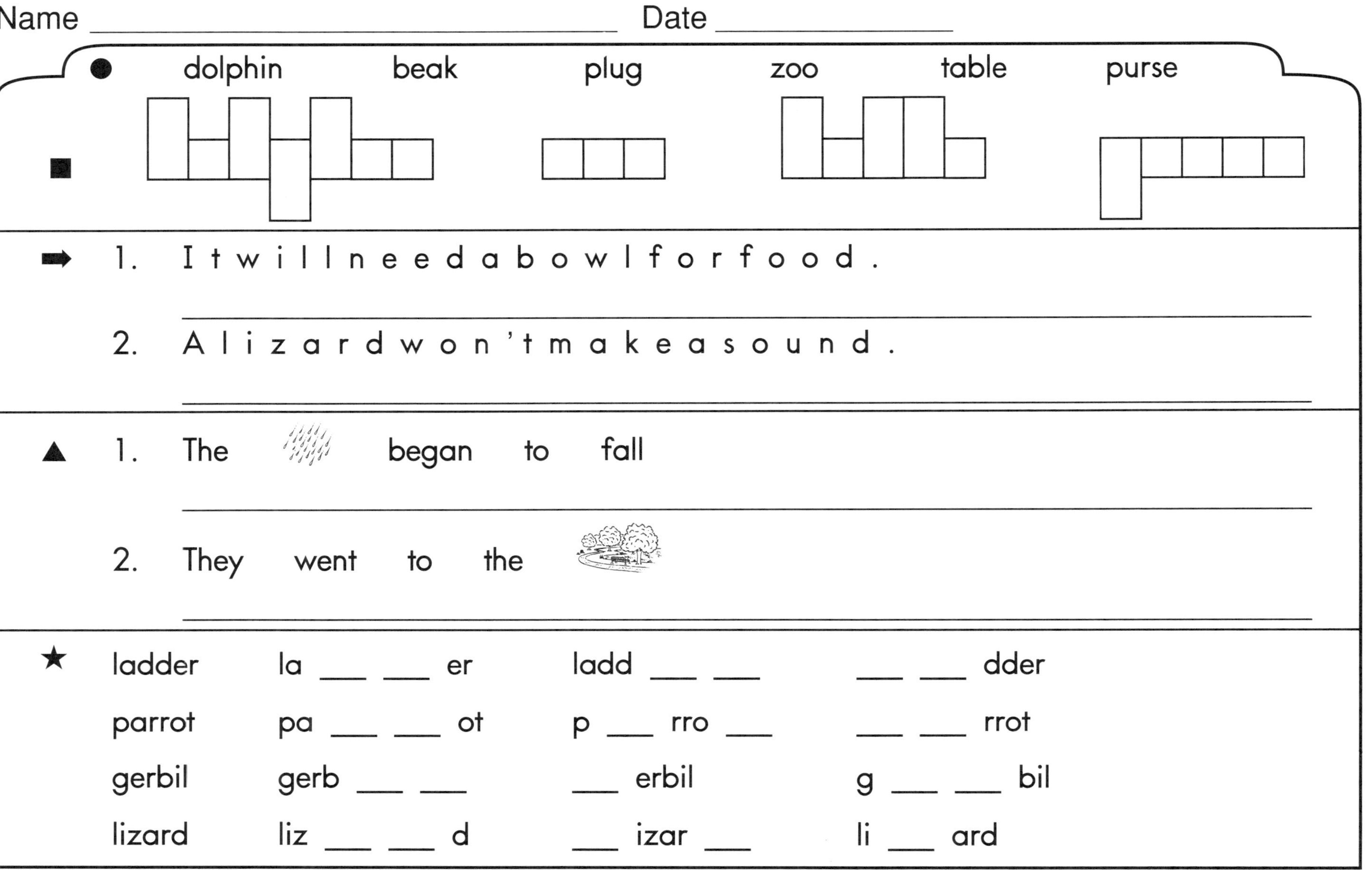

● dolphin beak plug zoo table purse

■

➡ 1. I t w i l l n e e d a b o w l f o r f o o d .

____

2. A l i z a r d w o n ' t m a k e a s o u n d .

____

▲ 1. The [rebus picture] began to fall

____

2. They went to the [rebus picture]

____

★

ladder	la ___ ___ er	ladd ___ ___	___ ___ dder
parrot	pa ___ ___ ot	p ___ rro ___	___ ___ rrot
gerbil	gerb ___ ___	___ erbil	g ___ ___ bil
lizard	liz ___ ___ d	___ izar ___	li ___ ard

● Have students read each word aloud and trace it. ■ Have students look at the shape of the boxes. Have them find a word that matches the shape and print the word in the boxes. ➡ Students should run a finger under the letters until a word is found. Have them put a mark between the words. They should then write the sentence on the line, leaving a space the size of a pencil between each word. ▲ Have students write the sentences using the written form of the word indicated by the rebus **picture** and adding punctuation. ★ Have the students write the missing letters. See the Answer Key on page 33.

Name ______________________ Date ______________

1. O bee O bear O beak	**7.** O eagle O ear O eat	**13.** O put O park O rake	**19.** O shell O well O sell
2. O been O bench O bit	**8.** O rat O get O gerbil	**14.** O parrot O part O pop	**20.** O swim O win O swing
3. O bell O bee O bowl	**9.** O gold O fish O goldfish	**15.** O rug O pine O plug	**21.** O tab O table O blue
4. O care O cage O bed	**10.** O bad O ladder O had	**16.** O pool O purse O pole	**22.** O tank O took O take
5. O cat O boot O castle	**11.** O lizard O zoo O like	**17.** O rake O river O rain	**23.** O to O toad O and
6. O done O dolphin O dog	**12.** O moon O key O monkey	**18.** O spy O school O spoon	**24.** O under O umbrella O other

See the Answer Key on page 33 to find which words to read aloud.

Name ______________________ Date ____________

Look at the words.
Circle things that are alive or can grow.
Underline things to wear.
Put a ★ star by things you find at home to use.
Draw a box around things too big for your house.
Words may be used more than one time.

basket		shark
beach		sled
blanket	gloves	tiger
boots	grasshopper	vine
chair	hose	volcano
crown	lion	wave
elephant	mountains	world
firefighter	octopus	yo-yo
flashlight	seahorse	zebra

See the Answer Key on page 33.

Name ________________________ Date ______________

Unit 2
To See the World

Lee and His Brother

Lee was reading a book about a grasshopper. His brother was sitting in a chair. He played with a yo-yo.

"Let's go for a ride on our bikes!" said Lee.

"Okay," said his little brother. Off they went.

"Wait!" called their mother. "Lunch will be ready soon."

Lee rode back to the yard. His brother came, too.

"One day, I will see the world," said Lee. "I will go as fast as that." He snapped his fingers.

The Trip Begins

"Is the world very big?" asked Lee's brother.

"Yes, the world is very, very big," said Lee. "First, I will see the tallest mountains. You can come with me."

"Will there be ice and snow?" asked his brother.

"Yes, it will be freezing cold," said Lee. "But we will stay warm. We will wear boots and gloves. And we will wear hats, too."

"How will we get by all that ice?" his brother asked.

"That's easy," said Lee. "We will have a racing sled. We will get over those mountains as fast as that." Lee snapped his fingers.

An Ocean Visit

"What will we see after we sled out of the mountains?" asked Lee's brother.

"We will see the biggest ocean in the world," said Lee. "We will have to cross it. The ocean will have a mean shark and a giant octopus. They will chase us all the way."

"Oh, no!" cried his brother.

"But we will be safe," said Lee. "A magic seahorse will carry us up out of the water. We will ride on its head. It will keep the shark and the octopus away with its tail."

"Then, we will be safe," said his brother.

"No," said Lee. "A giant whale will eat us up. I will have a flashlight. We will find the whale's blowhole. We will get out as fast as that." Lee snapped his fingers.

A Jungle Visit

"What in the world will we see after we leave the ocean?" asked Lee's brother.

"We will see a deep, dark jungle!" cried Lee.

"Oh, I am glad you have a flashlight," said his brother.

Lee said, "We will see a lion and a tiger. They will have big teeth. They will growl at us. But I will not be afraid of them."

"You won't?" asked his brother.

"No," said Lee. "We will be riding on my elephant. I will play my bugle. The lion and tiger will like my music."

"Will the animals forget to eat us?" asked Lee's brother.

"Yes," answered Lee. "Then, all the animals in the jungle will dance. Even the zebra will dance. We will grab a vine. We will swing away as fast as that!" Lee snapped his fingers.

An Island Visit

"Have we seen all the world yet?" asked Lee's brother.

"No," said Lee. "We swing on the vine to an island. We stop by a house. It is on fire. Hot lava from a volcano started the fire."

"Oh!" said his brother.

"But we will be safe," said Lee. "We will show the fire to the firefighter. He will try to put it out. The fire won't go out, though."

"This is scary!" said Lee's brother.

"Not for me," said Lee. "I will put on my fire hat and help the firefighter. I will get out my giant water hose. I will stop the fire as fast as that!" Lee snapped his fingers.

"Then, the firefighter will give me a crown. I will be the king!"

Back Home

"Now have we seen all the world?" asked Lee's brother.

"Not yet," said Lee. "I put on my crown. Then, we go for a swim at the beach. There is a giant wave coming toward us! We jump on an empty turtle shell. We ride the giant wave back to the beach."

Someone called to the boys. Lee and his brother saw a basket on the chair nearby. There was a very good smell coming from the basket.

"Now we have seen all the world," said Lee. "We are very hungry, too! So we find a basket of very good food to eat!"

"And look!" said his brother. "We find our mother."

Their mother put a blanket on the ground. They all sat down to eat. It felt good to be back home.

Name ______________________ Date ______________

● chair lion vine volcano crown tiger

■ [ ][ ][ ][ ][ ] [ ][ ][ ][ ] [ ][ ][ ][ ][ ] [ ][ ][ ][ ][ ]

➡ 1. E v e n t h e z e b r a w i l l d a n c e .

____

2. W e w i l l s h o w t h e f i r e t o t h e f i r e f i g h t e r .

____

▲ 1. We will have a racing

____

2. There is a giant coming toward us

____

★			
world	___ orld	w ___ ___ ld	wor ___ ___
gloves	___ ___ oves	gl ___ ves	glov ___ s
shark	sh ___ ___ k	___ ___ ark	shar ___
beach	___ each	b ___ ___ ch	bea ___ ___

● Have students read each word aloud and trace it. ■ Have students look at the shape of the boxes. Have them find a word that matches the shape and print the word in the boxes. ➡ Students should run a finger under the letters until a word is found. Have them put a mark between the words. They should then write the sentence on the line, leaving a space the size of a pencil between each word. ▲ Have students write the sentences using the written form of the word indicated by the rebus picture and adding punctuation. ★ Have the students write the missing letters. See the Answer Key on page 33.

Name ______________________ Date ______________

1. O chair O basket O barn	**7.** O goes O glow O gloves	**13.** O line O lion O ink	**19.** O fire O man O firefighter
2. O green O grasshopper O grass	**8.** O side O sit O sled	**14.** O zoo O sock O zebra	**20.** O he O so O hose
3. O yes O yo-yo O you	**9.** O octopus O open O top	**15.** O tent O tail O tiger	**21.** O crown O down O cow
4. O will O world O wide	**10.** O she O shark O park	**16.** O eat O elephant O tea	**22.** O each O beach O peach
5. O may O mountains O more	**11.** O horse O seahorse O shoe	**17.** O fine O mine O vine	**23.** O ask O basket O best
6. O boots O bites O blows	**12.** O flash O light O flashlight	**18.** O old O volcano O can	**24.** O blank O been O blanket

See the Answer Key on page 33 to find which words to read aloud.

Name ______________________________ Date ______________

Look at the words.
Circle things you can ride.
Underline things you can hold in your hands.
Put a ★ star by things that can make sounds.
Draw a box around things you find in the sky.
Words may be used more than one time.

balloons

basketball

bowling ball

candle

carrots

clouds

clown

cookies

flute

football

guitar

harp

horn

horse

juice

lightning

piano

plane

potato

rainbow

sailboat

soccer ball

spoon

tractor

truck

See the Answer Key on page 33.

Name ______________________ Date ____________

Super Soup

Reed went to Mandy's house to play. They made some soup. First, they put some water in a pot. Then, Mandy got some carrots. Reed put a cut potato in the pot. The water in the pot began to get very hot. Reed and Mandy stirred the soup. They had to use a very big spoon.

Mandy's mother said, "I smell something good!"

"Try to guess what we made," said Reed.

"Well," said Mandy's mother. "It smells like soup. Am I right?"

"Yes, you are right," said Mandy and Reed. "It is super soup!"

"I have some cookies," said Mandy's mother. "Do you think they will go with your super soup?"

"Oh, yes," said Mandy and Reed. "They will be just right!"

Sports

Emil likes to play basketball. He plays with a team called the Tigers. They have a lot of fun. When their game is over, they eat cookies and milk.

Tiffany plays soccer. She can kick the ball high in the air. She is on a team called the Stars. Last year, the Stars won the most games.

Chin likes to play football. He can throw the ball a long way. Sometimes, his dad likes to play with him. They have fun together.

Tiffany and her friends like to go bowling. She rolls the ball to hit the pins. She likes to knock them all down. Tiffany takes turns with her friends.

There are many games to play for fun. Which game do you like to play?

Parade

It was a hot summer day. People stood on the sidewalk. They looked down the street. They could see a clown. The clown had some balloons. There were many colors of balloons.

Another clown came closer and closer. He had three soccer balls. He could hold all the balls up in the air on his nose! The people clapped.

Next, they saw a horse. A lady sat on top of the horse. She threw candy to the people.

Music was playing. It was still hot. The people got thirsty. They had some juice to drink. It was good and cold. This was a fun parade.

Ways to Go

There are many ways to go places. Some people go places in a boat. Some boats are big. Some are small. A sailboat is a small boat. The wind makes a sailboat go.

A tractor can go across a farm. It helps to do the work. A horse used to do the farm work. A can do the work faster.

A truck can go on a farm. It can go in a city. A truck can go many places. It can help people to do work. It can do many things.

Some people like to go in a plane. A plane can go very fast. It can fly in the air and go far away. Many people can ride on a plane together.

Music for Sara

Sara and her dad went to the music store. They rode to town in the truck. Sara wanted to get a flute. Sara liked flute music.

Inside the store, she saw a piano. She tried to play it. It was so big! It would not fit in her room at home.

Then, Sara saw a guitar. She picked it up. She tried to play it. It was too big for her to hold.

Next, Sara tried a horn. She blew and blew. Her lips got very tired.

Sara played a harp next. It made very nice music. She did not want the harp, though. She knew what she wanted.

The flute was what Sara wanted. At last, she held one in her hands. She blew. It made good music. Sara was very happy with the flute.

At the Beach

Sari lived by the beach. Her friend, Pat, came over to play. It was raining. Sari played her piano for Pat. She played a song about the rain. She and Pat wanted the rain to go away.

They looked out the window. They saw some clouds in the sky. They saw some lightning. Then, a loud noise came. Now, it was dark inside. The lights were out. Sari got out a candle. Now, it was not so dark.

Then, the rain stopped. The clouds were gone. They could see the sun come out. Soon there was a rainbow.

Now, they could go out to play. It was fun to play in the sand at last.

Name ____________________ Date ____________

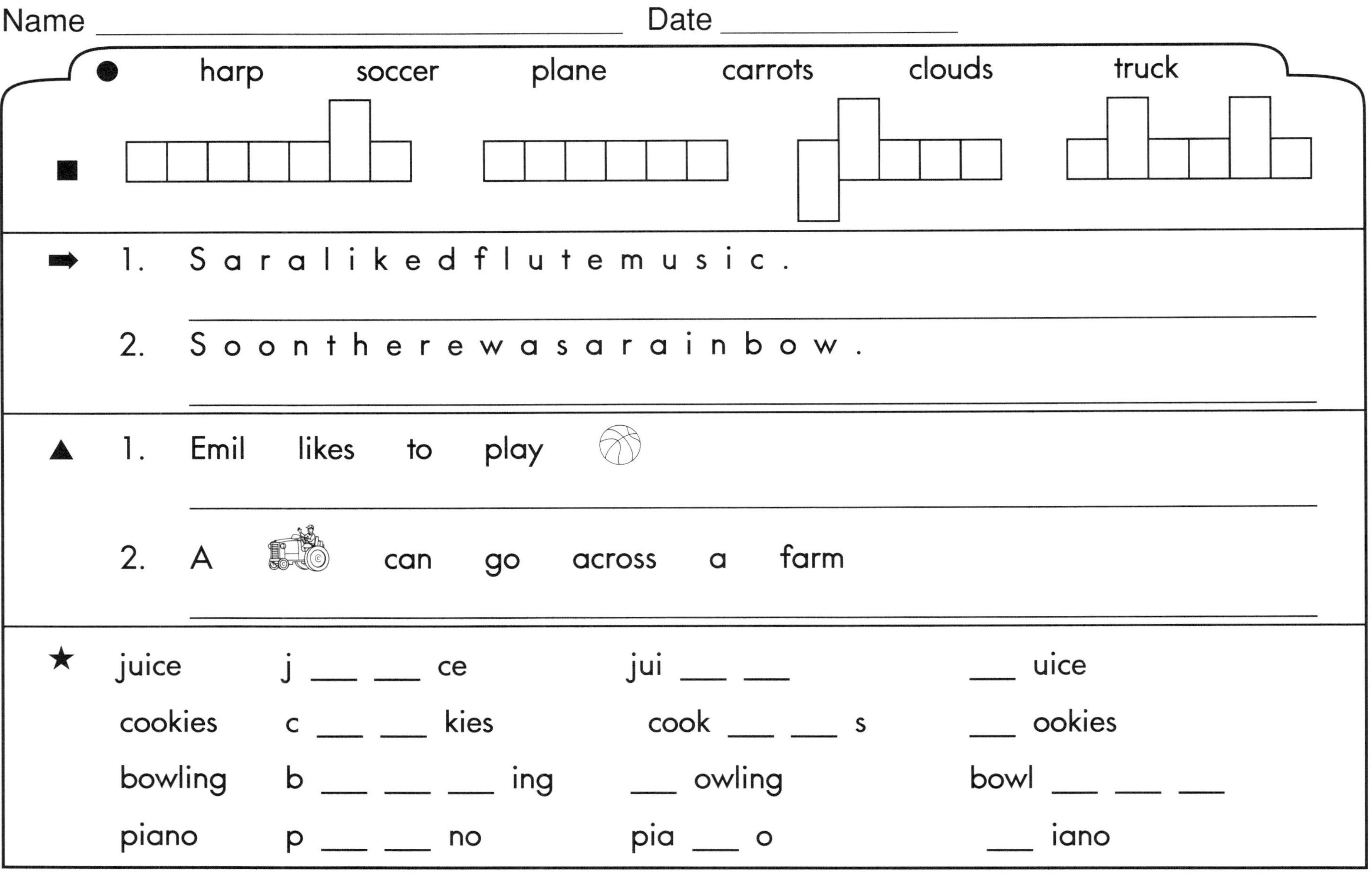

● harp soccer plane carrots clouds truck

■

➡ 1. S a r a l i k e d f l u t e m u s i c .

____

2. S o o n t h e r e w a s a r a i n b o w .

____

▲ 1. Emil likes to play

____

2. A can go across a farm

____

★ juice	j ___ ___ ce	jui ___ ___	___ uice
cookies	c ___ ___ kies	cook ___ ___ s	___ ookies
bowling	b ___ ___ ___ ing	___ owling	bowl ___ ___ ___
piano	p ___ ___ no	pia ___ o	___ iano

● Have students read each word aloud and trace it. ■ Have students look at the shape of the boxes. Have them find a word that matches the shape and print the word in the boxes. ➡ Students should run a finger under the letters until a word is found. Have them put a mark between the words. They should then write the sentence on the line, leaving a space the size of a pencil between each word. ▲ Have students write the sentences using the written form of the word indicated by the rebus picture and adding punctuation. ★ Have the students write the missing letters. See the Answer Key on page 33.

Name ______________________ Date ______________

1. O ball O loud O balloons	**7.** O low O clown O now	**13.** O are O sharp O harp	**19.** O potato O pot O boat
2. O basket O ball O basketball	**8.** O cook O clock O cookies	**14.** O horn O corn O torn	**20.** O bow O rain O rainbow
3. O bowling O bowl O owl	**9.** O horse O hurt O hands	**15.** O jet O just O juice	**21.** O sail O sailboat O boat
4. O candle O can O candy	**10.** O flute O fit O fill	**16.** O light O lightning O sing	**22.** O sock O soccer O soup
5. O car O carrots O cart	**11.** O foot O ball O football	**17.** O pan O piano O pin	**23.** O tractor O act O tack
6. O call O clouds O loud	**12.** O tar O guitar O tree	**18.** O plan O plane O pan	**24.** O tick O tock O truck

See the Answer Key on page 33 to find which words to read aloud.

beak	bench	bowl	cage	castle	dolphin	eagle
parrot	park	monkey	lizard	ladder	goldfish	gerbil
plug	purse	rain	school	shell	swing	table
chair	blanket	beach	basket	umbrella	toad	tank
crown	elephant	firefighter	flashlight	gloves	grasshopper	hose
vine	tiger	shark	seahorse	octopus	mountains	lion
volcano	wave	world	zebra	balloons	basketball	bowling
flute	horse	cookies	clown	clouds	carrots	candle
football	guitar	horn	juice	lightning	piano	plane
truck	tractor	spoon	soccer	sailboat	rainbow	potato

Students will paste a copy of this page onto construction paper and cut out the dominoes along the dotted lines. The first player will match two words end to end and read the matching word. The students can then color matching words the same color. The next player matches a word that has been played and reads the word.

potato	rainbow	sailboat	soccer	spoon	tractor	truck
plane	piano	lightning	juice	horn	guitar	football
candle	carrots	clouds	clown	cookies	horse	flute
bowling	basketball	balloons	zebra	world	wave	volcano
lion	mountains	octopus	seahorse	shark	tiger	vine
hose	grasshopper	gloves	flashlight	firefighter	elephant	crown
tank	toad	umbrella	basket	beach	blanket	chair
table	swing	shell	school	rain	purse	plug
gerbil	goldfish	ladder	lizard	monkey	park	parrot
eagle	dolphin	castle	cage	bowl	bench	beak

Students will paste a copy of this page onto construction paper and cut out the dominoes along the dotted lines. The first player will match two words end to end and read the matching word. The students can then color matching words the same color. The next player matches a word that has been played and reads the word.